We ho
this journ... and remember
your journey starts here

If you can spare a few moments, please leave us a review.
We are very interested in your feedback to create even better
products for you to enjoy in the near future.

Visit our website at amazing-notebooks.com or scan the QR code
below to see all of our awesome and creative products!

Thank you very much!

Amazing Notebooks

www.amazing-notebooks.com

Copyright © 2019. All rights reserved.

Dear Mom,

I will always love you and miss you with all my heart

...

Until we meet again.

_____

_____

_____

_____

_____

_____

_____

_____

I will love you forever Mom

Daily thoughts:

I will always love you and miss you with all my heart…

Today I remembered:

_____
_____
_____
_____

I wish I could tell you:

_____
_____
_____
_____

I am grateful for:

_____
_____

Today it was very hard to:

_____
_____
_____
_____

I will always love you and miss you with all my heart…

Daily thoughts:

_____

_____

_____

_____

_____

_____

_____

_____

_____

_____

_____

_____

_____

I will always love you and miss you with all my heart…

Today I remembered:

_____

_____

_____

_____

I wish I could tell you:

_____

_____

_____

_____

_____

I am grateful for:

_____

_____

Today it was very hard to:

_____

_____

_____

_____

I will always love you and miss you with all my heart…

Daily thoughts:

_____

_____

_____

_____

_____

_____

_____

_____

_____

_____

_____

_____

_____

_____

_____

_____

I will always love you and miss you with all my heart…

Today I remembered:

I wish I could tell you:

I am grateful for:

Today it was very hard to:

I will always love you and miss you with all my heart…

Daily thoughts:

I will always love you and miss you with all my heart…

Today I remembered:

_____
_____
_____
_____

I wish I could tell you:

_____
_____
_____
_____
_____

I am grateful for:

_____
_____
_____

Today it was very hard to:

_____
_____
_____
_____

I will always love you and miss you with all my heart…

Daily thoughts:

I will always love you and miss you with all my heart...

Today I remembered:

_____

_____

_____

_____

I wish I could tell you:

_____

_____

_____

_____

I am grateful for:

_____

_____

Today it was very hard to:

_____

_____

_____

I will always love you and miss you with all my heart...

Daily thoughts:

I will always love you and miss you with all my heart…

Today I remembered:

_____

_____

_____

_____

I wish I could tell you:

_____

_____

_____

_____

I am grateful for:

_____

_____

Today it was very hard to:

_____

_____

_____

I will always love you and miss you with all my heart...

Daily thoughts:

I will always love you and miss you with all my heart...

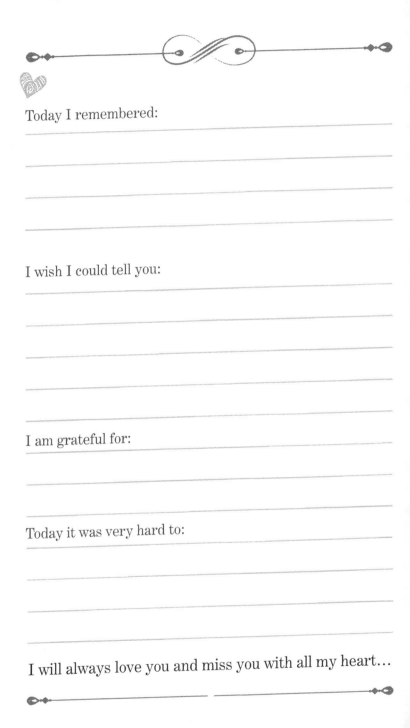

Today I remembered:

_____

_____

_____

_____

I wish I could tell you:

_____

_____

_____

_____

I am grateful for:

_____

_____

_____

Today it was very hard to:

_____

_____

_____

_____

I will always love you and miss you with all my heart…

Daily thoughts:

_____

_____

_____

_____

_____

_____

_____

_____

_____

_____

_____

_____

_____

I will always love you and miss you with all my heart...

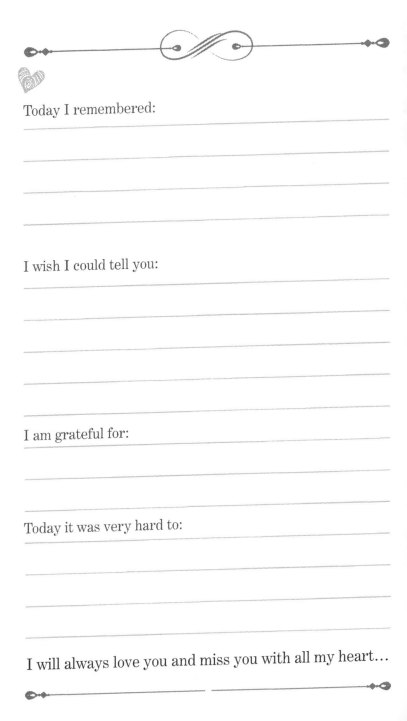

Today I remembered:

_____
_____
_____
_____

I wish I could tell you:

_____
_____
_____
_____

I am grateful for:

_____
_____

Today it was very hard to:

_____
_____
_____

I will always love you and miss you with all my heart…

Daily thoughts:

_____
_____
_____
_____
_____
_____
_____
_____
_____
_____
_____
_____
_____

I will always love you and miss you with all my heart…

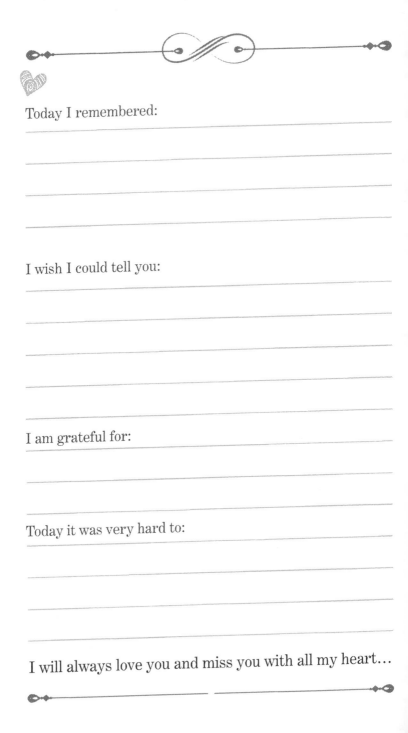

Today I remembered:

_____

_____

_____

_____

I wish I could tell you:

_____

_____

_____

_____

I am grateful for:

_____

_____

Today it was very hard to:

_____

_____

_____

_____

I will always love you and miss you with all my heart…

Daily thoughts:

_____

_____

_____

_____

_____

_____

_____

_____

_____

_____

_____

_____

_____

I will always love you and miss you with all my heart…

Today I remembered:

_____

_____

_____

_____

I wish I could tell you:

_____

_____

_____

_____

I am grateful for:

_____

_____

Today it was very hard to:

_____

_____

_____

I will always love you and miss you with all my heart…

Daily thoughts:

_____

_____

_____

_____

_____

_____

_____

_____

_____

_____

_____

_____

_____

_____

I will always love you and miss you with all my heart…

Today I remembered:

_____

_____

_____

_____

I wish I could tell you:

_____

_____

_____

_____

I am grateful for:

_____

_____

Today it was very hard to:

_____

_____

_____

I will always love you and miss you with all my heart…

Daily thoughts:

_____

_____

_____

_____

_____

_____

_____

_____

_____

_____

_____

_____

_____

_____

_____

_____

I will always love you and miss you with all my heart...

Today I remembered:

_____

_____

_____

_____

I wish I could tell you:

_____

_____

_____

_____

I am grateful for:

_____

_____

Today it was very hard to:

_____

_____

_____

I will always love you and miss you with all my heart...

Daily thoughts:

_____

_____

_____

_____

_____

_____

_____

_____

_____

_____

_____

_____

_____

_____

_____

I will always love you and miss you with all my heart...

Today I remembered:

_____

_____

_____

_____

I wish I could tell you:

_____

_____

_____

_____

I am grateful for:

_____

_____

Today it was very hard to:

_____

_____

_____

_____

I will always love you and miss you with all my heart…

Daily thoughts:

_____

_____

_____

_____

_____

_____

_____

_____

_____

_____

_____

_____

_____

_____

I will always love you and miss you with all my heart...

Today I remembered:

_____

_____

_____

_____

I wish I could tell you:

_____

_____

_____

_____

I am grateful for:

_____

_____

Today it was very hard to:

_____

_____

_____

I will always love you and miss you with all my heart…

Daily thoughts:

I will always love you and miss you with all my heart...

Today I remembered:

_____
_____
_____
_____

I wish I could tell you:

_____
_____
_____
_____

I am grateful for:

_____
_____

Today it was very hard to:

_____
_____
_____
_____

I will always love you and miss you with all my heart…

Daily thoughts:

_____

_____

_____

_____

_____

_____

_____

_____

_____

_____

_____

_____

_____

_____

I will always love you and miss you with all my heart…

Today I remembered:

_____

_____

_____

_____

I wish I could tell you:

_____

_____

_____

_____

I am grateful for:

_____

_____

Today it was very hard to:

_____

_____

_____

I will always love you and miss you with all my heart...

Daily thoughts:

_____

_____

_____

_____

_____

_____

_____

_____

_____

_____

_____

_____

_____

_____

I will always love you and miss you with all my heart...

Today I remembered:

_____

_____

_____

_____

I wish I could tell you:

_____

_____

_____

_____

I am grateful for:

_____

_____

Today it was very hard to:

_____

_____

_____

I will always love you and miss you with all my heart...

Daily thoughts:

I will always love you and miss you with all my heart…

Heart Designed by Freepik / Separator designed by rawpixel.com
Cover picture by jcomp / Freepik

Today I remembered:

_____
_____
_____
_____

I wish I could tell you:

_____
_____
_____
_____
_____

I am grateful for:

_____
_____

Today it was very hard to:

_____
_____
_____

I will always love you and miss you with all my heart…

Daily thoughts:

I will always love you and miss you with all my heart…

Today I remembered:

_____

_____

_____

_____

I wish I could tell you:

_____

_____

_____

_____

I am grateful for:

_____

_____

Today it was very hard to:

_____

_____

_____

_____

I will always love you and miss you with all my heart…

Daily thoughts:

_____

_____

_____

_____

_____

_____

_____

_____

_____

_____

_____

_____

_____

_____

I will always love you and miss you with all my heart...

Today I remembered:

I wish I could tell you:

I am grateful for:

Today it was very hard to:

I will always love you and miss you with all my heart...

Daily thoughts:

_____

_____

_____

_____

_____

_____

_____

_____

_____

_____

_____

_____

_____

_____

I will always love you and miss you with all my heart...

Today I remembered:

_____

_____

_____

_____

I wish I could tell you:

_____

_____

_____

_____

I am grateful for:

_____

_____

Today it was very hard to:

_____

_____

_____

_____

I will always love you and miss you with all my heart…

Daily thoughts:

I will always love you and miss you with all my heart...

Today I remembered:

_____

_____

_____

_____

I wish I could tell you:

_____

_____

_____

_____

I am grateful for:

_____

_____

_____

Today it was very hard to:

_____

_____

_____

_____

I will always love you and miss you with all my heart...

Daily thoughts:

I will always love you and miss you with all my heart…

Today I remembered:

_____

_____

_____

_____

I wish I could tell you:

_____

_____

_____

_____

I am grateful for:

_____

_____

Today it was very hard to:

_____

_____

_____

I will always love you and miss you with all my heart…

Daily thoughts:

_____

_____

_____

_____

_____

_____

_____

_____

_____

_____

_____

_____

_____

_____

I will always love you and miss you with all my heart...

Today I remembered:

_____

_____

_____

_____

I wish I could tell you:

_____

_____

_____

_____

I am grateful for:

_____

_____

Today it was very hard to:

_____

_____

_____

_____

I will always love you and miss you with all my heart…

Daily thoughts:

_____

_____

_____

_____

_____

_____

_____

_____

_____

_____

_____

_____

_____

_____

I will always love you and miss you with all my heart...

Today I remembered:

_____

_____

_____

_____

I wish I could tell you:

_____

_____

_____

_____

_____

I am grateful for:

_____

_____

Today it was very hard to:

_____

_____

_____

_____

I will always love you and miss you with all my heart...

Daily thoughts:

_____

_____

_____

_____

_____

_____

_____

_____

_____

_____

_____

_____

_____

_____

I will always love you and miss you with all my heart...

Today I remembered:

_____

_____

_____

_____

I wish I could tell you:

_____

_____

_____

_____

I am grateful for:

_____

_____

Today it was very hard to:

_____

_____

_____

I will always love you and miss you with all my heart...

Daily thoughts:

_____

_____

_____

_____

_____

_____

_____

_____

_____

_____

_____

_____

_____

_____

I will always love you and miss you with all my heart…

Today I remembered:

_____

_____

_____

_____

I wish I could tell you:

_____

_____

_____

_____

I am grateful for:

_____

_____

Today it was very hard to:

_____

_____

_____

I will always love you and miss you with all my heart…

Daily thoughts:

_____

_____

_____

_____

_____

_____

_____

_____

_____

_____

_____

_____

_____

_____

I will always love you and miss you with all my heart…

Today I remembered:

_____

_____

_____

_____

I wish I could tell you:

_____

_____

_____

_____

I am grateful for:

_____

_____

Today it was very hard to:

_____

_____

_____

I will always love you and miss you with all my heart…

Daily thoughts:

_____

_____

_____

_____

_____

_____

_____

_____

_____

_____

_____

_____

_____

I will always love you and miss you with all my heart…

Today I remembered:

_____

_____

_____

_____

I wish I could tell you:

_____

_____

_____

_____

I am grateful for:

_____

_____

_____

Today it was very hard to:

_____

_____

_____

_____

I will always love you and miss you with all my heart...

Daily thoughts:

I will always love you and miss you with all my heart...

Today I remembered:

_____
_____
_____
_____

I wish I could tell you:

_____
_____
_____
_____
_____

I am grateful for:

_____
_____
_____

Today it was very hard to:

_____
_____
_____
_____

I will always love you and miss you with all my heart...

Daily thoughts:

I will always love you and miss you with all my heart...

Today I remembered:

I wish I could tell you:

I am grateful for:

Today it was very hard to:

I will always love you and miss you with all my heart...

Daily thoughts:

_____

_____

_____

_____

_____

_____

_____

_____

_____

_____

_____

_____

_____

_____

I will always love you and miss you with all my heart...

Today I remembered:

_____

_____

_____

_____

I wish I could tell you:

_____

_____

_____

_____

I am grateful for:

_____

_____

Today it was very hard to:

_____

_____

_____

I will always love you and miss you with all my heart...

Daily thoughts:

_____

_____

_____

_____

_____

_____

_____

_____

_____

_____

_____

_____

_____

_____

I will always love you and miss you with all my heart...

Today I remembered:

_____

_____

_____

_____

I wish I could tell you:

_____

_____

_____

_____

I am grateful for:

_____

_____

Today it was very hard to:

_____

_____

_____

I will always love you and miss you with all my heart...

Daily thoughts:

_____

_____

_____

_____

_____

_____

_____

_____

_____

_____

_____

_____

_____

_____

I will always love you and miss you with all my heart...

Today I remembered:

_____

_____

_____

_____

I wish I could tell you:

_____

_____

_____

_____

I am grateful for:

_____

_____

Today it was very hard to:

_____

_____

_____

I will always love you and miss you with all my heart...

Daily thoughts:

I will always love you and miss you with all my heart...

Today I remembered:

_____

_____

_____

_____

I wish I could tell you:

_____

_____

_____

_____

I am grateful for:

_____

_____

Today it was very hard to:

_____

_____

_____

I will always love you and miss you with all my heart...

Daily thoughts:

_____

_____

_____

_____

_____

_____

_____

_____

_____

_____

_____

_____

_____

I will always love you and miss you with all my heart…

Heart Designed by Freepik / Separator designed by rawpixel.com
Cover picture by jcomp / Freepik

Today I remembered:

_____

_____

_____

_____

I wish I could tell you:

_____

_____

_____

_____

I am grateful for:

_____

_____

Today it was very hard to:

_____

_____

_____

I will always love you and miss you with all my heart...

Daily thoughts:

_____

_____

_____

_____

_____

_____

_____

_____

_____

_____

_____

_____

_____

_____

_____

_____

_____

_____

_____

I will always love you and miss you with all my heart...

Today I remembered:

_____
_____
_____
_____

I wish I could tell you:

_____
_____
_____
_____

I am grateful for:

_____
_____

Today it was very hard to:

_____
_____
_____

I will always love you and miss you with all my heart…

Daily thoughts:

_____

_____

_____

_____

_____

_____

_____

_____

_____

_____

_____

_____

_____

_____

I will always love you and miss you with all my heart...

Today I remembered:

_____

_____

_____

_____

I wish I could tell you:

_____

_____

_____

_____

_____

I am grateful for:

_____

_____

Today it was very hard to:

_____

_____

_____

_____

I will always love you and miss you with all my heart…

Daily thoughts:

_____

_____

_____

_____

_____

_____

_____

_____

_____

_____

_____

_____

_____

_____

_____

_____

_____

_____

_____

I will always love you and miss you with all my heart...

Today I remembered:

_____
_____
_____
_____

I wish I could tell you:

_____
_____
_____
_____
_____

I am grateful for:

_____
_____
_____

Today it was very hard to:

_____
_____
_____
_____

I will always love you and miss you with all my heart...

Daily thoughts:

_____

_____

_____

_____

_____

_____

_____

_____

_____

_____

_____

_____

_____

_____

_____

_____

I will always love you and miss you with all my heart…

Today I remembered:

_____

_____

_____

_____

I wish I could tell you:

_____

_____

_____

_____

_____

I am grateful for:

_____

_____

_____

Today it was very hard to:

_____

_____

_____

_____

I will always love you and miss you with all my heart...

Daily thoughts:

_____

_____

_____

_____

_____

_____

_____

_____

_____

_____

_____

_____

_____

_____

_____

_____

I will always love you and miss you with all my heart…

Today I remembered:

I wish I could tell you:

I am grateful for:

Today it was very hard to:

I will always love you and miss you with all my heart…

Daily thoughts:

_____

_____

_____

_____

_____

_____

_____

_____

_____

_____

_____

_____

_____

_____

_____

I will always love you and miss you with all my heart…

Today I remembered:

_____
_____
_____
_____

I wish I could tell you:

_____
_____
_____
_____

I am grateful for:

_____
_____

Today it was very hard to:

_____
_____
_____

I will always love you and miss you with all my heart...

Daily thoughts:

_____

_____

_____

_____

_____

_____

_____

_____

_____

_____

_____

_____

_____

_____

_____

_____

I will always love you and miss you with all my heart...

Today I remembered:

_____
_____
_____
_____

I wish I could tell you:

_____
_____
_____
_____
_____

I am grateful for:

_____
_____
_____

Today it was very hard to:

_____
_____
_____
_____

I will always love you and miss you with all my heart...

Daily thoughts:

_____

_____

_____

_____

_____

_____

_____

_____

_____

_____

_____

I will always love you and miss you with all my heart...

Today I remembered:

I wish I could tell you:

I am grateful for:

Today it was very hard to:

I will always love you and miss you with all my heart...

Daily thoughts:

I will always love you and miss you with all my heart...

Today I remembered:

I wish I could tell you:

I am grateful for:

Today it was very hard to:

I will always love you and miss you with all my heart...

Daily thoughts:

_____

_____

_____

_____

_____

_____

_____

_____

_____

_____

_____

_____

_____

_____

I will always love you and miss you with all my heart...

Today I remembered:

_____

_____

_____

_____

I wish I could tell you:

_____

_____

_____

_____

I am grateful for:

_____

_____

Today it was very hard to:

_____

_____

_____

I will always love you and miss you with all my heart...

Daily thoughts:

I will always love you and miss you with all my heart...

Today I remembered:

I wish I could tell you:

I am grateful for:

Today it was very hard to:

I will always love you and miss you with all my heart…

Daily thoughts:

_____

_____

_____

_____

_____

_____

_____

_____

_____

_____

_____

_____

_____

I will always love you and miss you with all my heart...

Today I remembered:

_____

_____

_____

_____

I wish I could tell you:

_____

_____

_____

_____

I am grateful for:

_____

_____

Today it was very hard to:

_____

_____

_____

I will always love you and miss you with all my heart...

Daily thoughts:

_____

_____

_____

_____

_____

_____

_____

_____

_____

_____

_____

_____

_____

_____

_____

_____

_____

_____

I will always love you and miss you with all my heart…

Today I remembered:

_____

_____

_____

_____

I wish I could tell you:

_____

_____

_____

_____

I am grateful for:

_____

_____

Today it was very hard to:

_____

_____

_____

I will always love you and miss you with all my heart…

Daily thoughts:

_____

_____

_____

_____

_____

_____

_____

_____

_____

_____

_____

_____

_____

I will always love you and miss you with all my heart…

Today I remembered:

_____

_____

_____

_____

I wish I could tell you:

_____

_____

_____

_____

I am grateful for:

_____

_____

Today it was very hard to:

_____

_____

_____

_____

I will always love you and miss you with all my heart...

Daily thoughts:

_____

_____

_____

_____

_____

_____

_____

_____

_____

_____

_____

_____

I will always love you and miss you with all my heart…

Today I remembered:

_____

_____

_____

_____

I wish I could tell you:

_____

_____

_____

_____

I am grateful for:

_____

_____

Today it was very hard to:

_____

_____

_____

I will always love you and miss you with all my heart…

Daily thoughts:

_____

_____

_____

_____

_____

_____

_____

_____

_____

_____

_____

_____

_____

_____

_____

_____

I will always love you and miss you with all my heart…

Today I remembered:

_____

_____

_____

_____

I wish I could tell you:

_____

_____

_____

_____

I am grateful for:

_____

_____

Today it was very hard to:

_____

_____

_____

I will always love you and miss you with all my heart...

Daily thoughts:

_____
_____
_____
_____
_____
_____
_____
_____
_____
_____
_____
_____
_____
_____
_____
_____

I will always love you and miss you with all my heart…

Today I remembered:

_____
_____
_____
_____

I wish I could tell you:

_____
_____
_____
_____

I am grateful for:

_____
_____

Today it was very hard to:

_____
_____
_____

I will always love you and miss you with all my heart…

Daily thoughts:

_____

_____

_____

_____

_____

_____

_____

_____

_____

_____

_____

_____

I will always love you and miss you with all my heart...

Today I remembered:

_____

_____

_____

_____

I wish I could tell you:

_____

_____

_____

_____

_____

I am grateful for:

_____

_____

Today it was very hard to:

_____

_____

_____

_____

I will always love you and miss you with all my heart...

Daily thoughts:

I will always love you and miss you with all my heart…

Today I remembered:

_____

_____

_____

_____

I wish I could tell you:

_____

_____

_____

_____

I am grateful for:

_____

_____

Today it was very hard to:

_____

_____

_____

I will always love you and miss you with all my heart...

Daily thoughts:

_____

_____

_____

_____

_____

_____

_____

_____

_____

_____

_____

_____

_____

_____

I will always love you and miss you with all my heart…

Today I remembered:

_____

_____

_____

_____

I wish I could tell you:

_____

_____

_____

_____

I am grateful for:

_____

_____

Today it was very hard to:

_____

_____

_____

I will always love you and miss you with all my heart...

Daily thoughts:

I will always love you and miss you with all my heart…

Today I remembered:

_____
_____
_____
_____

I wish I could tell you:

_____
_____
_____
_____
_____

I am grateful for:

_____
_____
_____

Today it was very hard to:

_____
_____
_____
_____

I will always love you and miss you with all my heart...

Daily thoughts:

_____

_____

_____

_____

_____

_____

_____

_____

_____

_____

_____

_____

_____

I will always love you and miss you with all my heart...

Today I remembered:

_____

_____

_____

_____

I wish I could tell you:

_____

_____

_____

_____

_____

I am grateful for:

_____

_____

Today it was very hard to:

_____

_____

_____

_____

I will always love you and miss you with all my heart…

Daily thoughts:

_____
_____
_____
_____
_____
_____
_____
_____
_____
_____
_____
_____
_____
_____
_____

I will always love you and miss you with all my heart…

Today I remembered:

_____

_____

_____

_____

I wish I could tell you:

_____

_____

_____

_____

I am grateful for:

_____

_____

Today it was very hard to:

_____

_____

_____

_____

I will always love you and miss you with all my heart...

Daily thoughts:

_____

_____

_____

_____

_____

_____

_____

_____

_____

_____

_____

_____

_____

I will always love you and miss you with all my heart…

Today I remembered:

_____

_____

_____

_____

I wish I could tell you:

_____

_____

_____

_____

I am grateful for:

_____

_____

Today it was very hard to:

_____

_____

_____

I will always love you and miss you with all my heart...

Daily thoughts:

_____

_____

_____

_____

_____

_____

_____

_____

_____

_____

_____

_____

_____

I will always love you and miss you with all my heart…

Today I remembered:

_____

_____

_____

_____

I wish I could tell you:

_____

_____

_____

_____

_____

I am grateful for:

_____

_____

Today it was very hard to:

_____

_____

_____

_____

I will always love you and miss you with all my heart...

Daily thoughts:

I will always love you and miss you with all my heart...

Today I remembered:

_____

_____

_____

_____

I wish I could tell you:

_____

_____

_____

_____

I am grateful for:

_____

_____

Today it was very hard to:

_____

_____

_____

I will always love you and miss you with all my heart...

Daily thoughts:

_____

_____

_____

_____

_____

_____

_____

_____

_____

_____

_____

_____

_____

_____

_____

I will always love you and miss you with all my heart…

Today I remembered:

_____

_____

_____

_____

I wish I could tell you:

_____

_____

_____

_____

_____

I am grateful for:

_____

_____

Today it was very hard to:

_____

_____

_____

_____

I will always love you and miss you with all my heart...

Daily thoughts:

_____

_____

_____

_____

_____

_____

_____

_____

_____

_____

_____

_____

_____

_____

_____

I will always love you and miss you with all my heart…

Today I remembered:

_____

_____

_____

_____

I wish I could tell you:

_____

_____

_____

_____

I am grateful for:

_____

_____

Today it was very hard to:

_____

_____

_____

I will always love you and miss you with all my heart…

Daily thoughts:

_____

_____

_____

_____

_____

_____

_____

_____

_____

_____

_____

_____

_____

_____

I will always love you and miss you with all my heart...

Today I remembered:

_____

_____

_____

_____

I wish I could tell you:

_____

_____

_____

_____

I am grateful for:

_____

_____

Today it was very hard to:

_____

_____

_____

I will always love you and miss you with all my heart...

Daily thoughts:

_____

_____

_____

_____

_____

_____

_____

_____

_____

_____

_____

_____

_____

I will always love you and miss you with all my heart...

Today I remembered:

_____

_____

_____

_____

I wish I could tell you:

_____

_____

_____

_____

I am grateful for:

_____

_____

Today it was very hard to:

_____

_____

_____

I will always love you and miss you with all my heart...

Daily thoughts:

_____

_____

_____

_____

_____

_____

_____

_____

_____

_____

_____

_____

_____

_____

I will always love you and miss you with all my heart…

Today I remembered:

_____

_____

_____

_____

I wish I could tell you:

_____

_____

_____

_____

_____

I am grateful for:

_____

_____

Today it was very hard to:

_____

_____

_____

_____

I will always love you and miss you with all my heart…

Daily thoughts:

I will always love you and miss you with all my heart...

We hope you`ll enjoy this journal and remember your journey starts here

If you can spare a few moments, please leave us a review.
We are very interested in your feedback to create even better
products for you to enjoy in the near future.

Visit our website at amazing-notebooks.com or scan the QR code
below to see all of our awesome and creative products!

Thank you very much!

Amazing Notebooks

www.amazing-notebooks.com

Copyright © 2019. All rights reserved.